Symbols of American Freedom

The Gateway Arch

by Chelsey Hankins

Series Consultant: Jerry D. Thompson,
Regents Professor of History,
Texas A&M International University

CHELSEA CLUBHOUSE
An Imprint of Chelsea House Publishers

Symbols of American Freedom: The Gateway Arch

Chelsea Clubhouse
An imprint of Chelsea House Publishers
132 West 31st Street
New York NY 10001

Library of Congress Cataloging-in-Publication Data
Hankins, Chelsey.
    The Gateway Arch / by Chelsey Hankins.
        p. cm. — (Symbols of American freedom)
    Includes index.
    ISBN 978-1-60413-513-8 (acid-free paper) 1. Gateway Arch (Saint Louis, Mo.)—Juvenile literature.
    2. Arches—Missouri—Saint Louis--Design and construction—Juvenile literature. 3. United States—
    Territorial expansion—Juvenile literature. I. Title. II. Series.
  TA660.A7H36 2010
  977.8'66—dc22
                                                          2009006913

Developed for Chelsea House by RJF Publishing LLC (www.RJFpublishing.com)
Text and cover design by Tammy West/Westgraphix LLC
Maps by Stefan Chabluk
Photo research by Edward A. Thomas
Index by Nila Glikin

Photo Credits: cover: Shutterstock Images; 4, 5, 41: Gateway Arch Riverfront; 6, 39: iStockphoto; 8: Picture Collection, The New York Public Library, Astor, Lenox and Tilden Foundations; 9: North Wind/North Wind Picture Archives; 11: © Bettmann/CORBIS; 12: AP/Wide World Photos; 16: © 1999 U.S. Mint; 17: © george-sanker.com/Alamy; 18: Library of Congress, U.S. Serial Set, Number 1054 House Executive Document 56, 36th Congress, 1st Session; 19: © Corbis; 21: Library of Congress LC-USZ62-730; 24, 27: Getty Images; 25: Courtesy of Laura Ingalls Wilder Home Association Mansfield, MO; 26: Library of Congress LC-DIG-ppmsca-08371; 28: Library of Congress LC-USZC4-2852; 31: Western Historical Manuscript Collection, University of Missouri-St. Louis; 33: Jefferson National Expansion Memorial/National Park Service; 34: Saarinen, Eero, Collection Manuscripts & Archives, Yale University/James Kilpatrick/The Detroit News; 36: © Bettmann/Corbis; 40: Library of Congress LC-USZ62-5092; 43: © PhotoStock-Israel/Alamy.

Table of Contents

Words that are defined in the Glossary are in **bold** type
the first time they appear in the text.

Chapter 1

Symbol of Westward Expansion

Located on the Mississippi River in St. Louis, Missouri, the **Gateway Arch** is a **monument** to the explorers and **pioneers** who settled the American West. Planned and built over a period of 30 years in the mid-20th century, the Arch is part of what is known as a **national memorial**—a place that is important to the United States because it has historic value. Standing 630 feet (192 meters) high, the Arch is the tallest monument in the United States—taller than such other famous monuments as the Statue of Liberty in New York or the Washington Monument in Washington, D.C.

A Simple Design

The Gateway Arch is famous for its simple design. It actually looks like a gateway that people could have traveled through to start their journey

The lights of the Gateway Arch and city of St. Louis are reflected in the Mississippi River.

305 feet/
93 meters

555 feet/
169 meters

630 feet/
192 meters

Statue of
Liberty

Washington
Monument

Gateway Arch

Quick Facts About the Arch

Height: 630 feet (192 meters)

Width at base: 630 feet (192 meters)

Thickness at base: 54 feet (16 meters)

Thickness at top: 17 feet (5 meters)

Made of: stainless steel and concrete

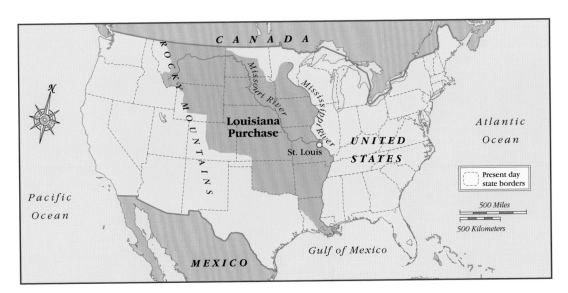

In 1803, the United States made the Louisiana Purchase from France, and during the 1800s, many Americans moved west. St. Louis's location on the Mississippi River and near the Missouri River made the city an ideal gateway to the West for explorers, fur traders, and settlers.

west. The sides of the Arch are much thicker at the base than they are at the top. The shape of the arch is called an **inverted catenary curve**. An inverted catenary curve is the name for the shape that a chain would take if you held it upside down—that is, held it in the middle and let the two sides hang down. The distance on the ground from one end of the arch to the other is also 630 feet (192 meters)—the same as the height.

A Fitting Location

The city of St. Louis is a fitting location for the Arch. In 1803, in the Louisiana Purchase, the United States bought from France a vast amount of land. From east to west, the Louisiana Purchase stretched between the Mississippi River and the Rocky Mountains. From north to south, it went from what is today Canada to the Gulf of Mexico. In 1804, when the explorers Meriwether Lewis and William Clark set out to explore the new

The City of St. Louis

St. Louis is located on the west bank of the Mississippi River, just below where the Missouri River comes into the Mississippi. It started as a trading post, set up by French fur traders in 1764. Since the site is near two of North America's largest rivers, it was easy for Native Americans to travel by water to bring furs there. It was also easy for the French traders to take the furs away.

St. Louis became part of the United States in the Louisiana Purchase of 1803. The city grew in the 1800s and early 1900s. It was an important starting point for people going West and then for railroads to the West. It was a major port on the Mississippi River, and many factories opened in the city. Today, St. Louis has about 350,000 people and is the second-largest city in Missouri (after Kansas City). It continues to benefit from its location on the Mississippi River, and about 1 million people a year come to visit the Gateway Arch.

French fur traders clear the land and build a trading post at what is now St. Louis.

Fur traders, such as these men loading their boat with animal furs, were among the first people to move into the land explored by Lewis and Clark.

territory and beyond, they started their historic **expedition** from a camp just outside St. Louis.

In the decades that followed, many thousands of fur traders, settlers going to the Northwest over the Oregon Trail, people heading to California in the 1849 Gold Rush, and other pioneers passed through St. Louis and the rest of Missouri on their way west. The settlers braved a long journey, rough roads, bad weather, shortages of food and water, sickness, and loneliness. But most completed the trip, started new towns and farms, and began a new life. Their hard work and bravery helped to make the United States the country it is today.

The Lewis and Clark Expedition

In the early 1800s, the size of the United States was very different from what it is today. The western boundary of the **continental United States**, which today reaches all the way to the Pacific Ocean, then stretched only to the Mississippi River. France, Spain, and Great Britain controlled the land west of the Mississippi River. A major step in expanding the size of the United States took place in 1803 when President Thomas Jefferson decided that the United States should buy the Louisiana Territory from France. This vast territory extended from the Gulf of Mexico north to Canada and from the Mississippi River to as far west as the Rocky Mountains. Because of war in Europe, France needed money, and it agreed to sell the 828,000 square miles (2,145,000 square kilometers) of land for about $15 million. For less than 3 cents an acre—a bargain, even at that time—Jefferson's purchase doubled the size of the United States.

Sacagawea, a Native American woman, helped guide the Lewis and Clark Expedition as it explored the Louisiana Purchase.

Eventually, all or part of thirteen U.S. states would be formed out of the Louisiana Territory. It included forests and land that could be used for farming and ranching. Native Americans lived throughout the territory, but most of it was unknown to Americans living east of the Mississippi River. Jefferson decided that he needed to send a group of explorers to find out more about at least part of the land the United States had just bought.

Jefferson and Meriwether Lewis

President Jefferson picked his own personal secretary, Meriwether Lewis, to lead an expedition that would travel by boat, going north and west up the Missouri River to explore the northern part of the new territory. (Traveling by boat at that time in **wilderness** areas was generally much easier than traveling by land.) Lewis had been a U.S. Army officer until going to work

President Thomas Jefferson doubled the size of the United States when he made the Louisiana Purchase in 1803.

for Jefferson in 1801. Jefferson asked Lewis to keep a journal in which he would describe the trip and the things he saw, so that other people could read about them. He wanted Lewis to keep careful records of the animals and plants that he found during his journey. And Jefferson asked Lewis to meet with the Native Americans living on the land.

Finally, Jefferson hoped that Lewis's expedition would find a so-called Northwest Passage, a water route that would connect the eastern United States and the Pacific Ocean and make it easier for people and goods to move by water across the country. To do this, Lewis would have to go farther west than the boundary of the Louisiana Purchase. Jefferson mentioned the Northwest Passage in his instructions to Lewis:

> "The object of your mission is to explore the Missouri River, and such principal stream of it, as, by its course and communication with the water of the Pacific Ocean may offer the most direct and practicable water [route] across this continent for the purposes of commerce."

Who Really Owned the Land?

Although France (and at times other European nations) claimed the land of the Louisiana Territory, Native Americans had lived for thousands of years on this land. They were not included in the talks with France in which the United States bought the Louisiana Territory. Later, they did not give their permission for their land to be taken over by settlers from the United States. The growth of the United States often came at the expense of Native Americans, who lost their homelands and traditional ways of life and were forced to move to **reservations**.

Jefferson had high hopes that the expedition would prove that his decision to spend $15 million on the Louisiana Purchase had been a wise one. He would continue to be in favor of expanding the territory of the United States, because he believed that expansion was the surest way to make the United States an important, wealthy nation.

The Expedition Begins

After he agreed to lead the expedition, Lewis asked William Clark to become co-leader with him. Clark was a former soldier, and he and Lewis had served together. Lewis and Clark set off on their journey in May 1804. They started with three boats, a crew of almost 50 men (most of them were soldiers, but the group also included Clark's black slave, York), a great deal of food and other supplies, and Lewis's Newfoundland dog, named Seaman. The expedition, called the "Corps of Discovery," left from a camp just outside St. Louis.

The men in the Corps of Discovery traveled for months before stopping near present-day Bismarck, North Dakota, for the winter. They decided

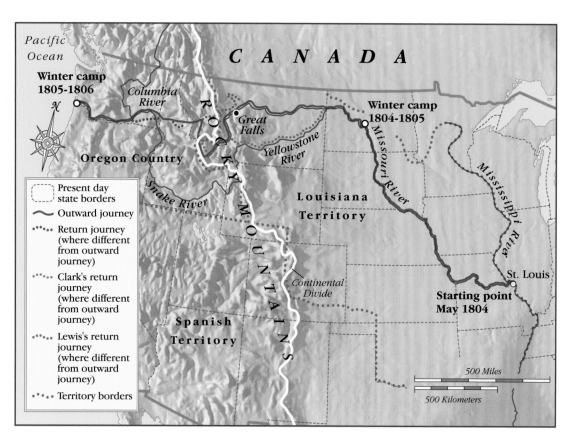

The map shows the route Lewis and Clark followed as they explored the Louisiana Territory, crossed the Rocky Mountains, and continued on to the Pacific Ocean. On their way back, the two men took different routes for part of the journey, in order to explore more of the land in the Louisiana Territory that now belonged to the United States.

to stay with two tribes, the Mandan and the Hidatsa, that lived in villages near the Missouri River. It was in these villages that Lewis and Clark first met Sacagawea, a Shoshone Indian, and her husband, Toussaint Charbonneau, a French Canadian trader. Lewis and Clark hired them as interpreters, to talk with Native Americans the expedition would meet when it moved farther west. (The Shoshone tribe lived in the Far West.) Sacagawea gave birth to a baby boy that winter, and he also went with them on their journey.

Crossing the Rockies

In the spring of 1805, the expedition began to move farther west up the Missouri River in a small group of canoes and boats. One of the original boats had already been sent back to St. Louis to report on how the trip was going so far.

One of the greatest surprises for the members of the Corps of Discovery as they continued west was their first glimpse of the massive and rugged Rocky Mountains. Parts of the Rockies are thousands of feet taller than any mountains in the eastern United States. Most members of the expedition had never in their lives seen mountains like these. Lewis and Clark also discovered that there was no Northwest Passage that they could use to travel by water through the mountains. They would have to travel overland to cross the Rockies (and to cross what is known as the Continental Divide).

Lewis and Clark were not well-prepared for this part of their journey. But even though there was already snow in the Rocky Mountains, they completed the crossing successfully in September of 1805 after Sacagawea convinced the Shoshone to provide the expedition with horses. On this part of the journey, the explorers saw grizzly bears, bighorn sheep, and other animals unknown to people in the eastern United States.

The Continental Divide

The Continental Divide, or Great Divide, is an imaginary line running from north to south in western North America. It runs along the **crest**, or highest peaks, of the Rocky Mountains. On the east side of the divide, rivers (like the Missouri River) flow toward the east, to the Atlantic Ocean and Gulf of Mexico. On the west side of the divide, rivers (like the Columbia River) flow toward the west and the Pacific Ocean.

To the Pacific and Home

After the difficult crossing of the Rockies, the expedition was fortunate to encounter the friendly Nez Perce tribe when it reached the **prairie** on the western side of the mountains. From the Nez Perce the expedition could get food and other supplies. Lewis and Clark were now outside the territory of the Louisiana Purchase. They continued their journey west by boat, traveling mostly down the Snake and Columbia rivers. A year and a half

Sacagawea, More Than an Interpreter

Sacagawea was only a young girl when she was kidnapped from her people, the Shoshone, and taken to live far away in the Hidatsa village where Lewis and Clark first met her years later. Lewis and Clark at first wanted only her husband to be their interpreter. They later decided that Sacagawea should also join the expedition because she would be able to talk with the Shoshone and other Native American tribes they were likely to come in contact with.

Sacagawea proved to be very valuable to Lewis and Clark. Her presence often calmed Native Americans when they first saw the expedition. They trusted her more than they trusted the white men who were with her. Because she knew how to live in the wilderness, she was able to find food that was safe to eat, and she made clothes that kept everyone warm. She also helped Lewis and Clark to trade with the Shoshone. Without her presence, it is doubtful that the Shoshone would have been friendly to white explorers crossing their land.

To honor Sacagawea, the U.S. Mint put a picture of her with her son on a $1 coin.

after they set out, they finally reached the Pacific Ocean, at a spot near present-day Astoria, Oregon, in November 1805.

After spending a cold rainy winter on the Pacific coast, the expedition began the journey back to St. Louis in March 1806. Lewis and Clark took a slightly different route back (Native Americans showed them a shorter way through the Rockies), and they even split up for a time in order to explore more territory. In September 1806—more than two years after the expedi-

tion started and having covered a total distance of about 8,000 miles (12,800 kilometers)—the members of the Corps of Discovery returned to St. Louis at the end of their long and amazing journey.

After the Expedition

Lewis and Clark were greeted by the people of St. Louis with a huge celebration. Congress gave both men double the pay they had been promised. Lewis was named governor of the Upper Louisiana Territory, an area that included parts of present-day Missouri and

Many members of the Lewis and Clark expedition saw grizzly bears for the first time as they explored the Louisiana Territory.

In Their Own Words

Lewis Describes the Great Falls

As they made their journey west, Lewis and Clark were often amazed by natural wonders they saw. When he first came upon the powerful waterfalls now known as the Great Falls of the Missouri River (in present-day Montana), Lewis described them this way in his journal:

"Hearing a tremendous roaring above me, I continued my route across the point of a hill…and was…presented by one of the most beautiful objects in nature, a cascade [waterfall] of about 50 feet [tall] stretching…across the river from side to side to the distance of at least a quarter of a mile. There the river pitches over a shelving rock, with an edge as regular and as straight as if formed by art.…The water descends in one even and uninterrupted sheet to the bottom where dashing against the rocky bottom [it] rises into foaming billows of great height and rapidly glides away, hissing, flashing, and sparkling as it departs."

An illustration of the Great Falls of the Missouri River.

Oklahoma, and Clark was made an **agent** to handle government relations with Native Americans.

Clark's maps of the West, which were printed in the 1810s, were used for the next thirty years by settlers traveling west. The journals of the Lewis and Clark expedition were first published in 1814. People still read them today to learn about the expedition and what it discovered.

Lewis and Clark's exploration of the Pacific Northwest—the area west of the Rockies and west of the Louisiana Purchase—was a basis for the U.S. government to claim that territory as part of the United States.

Clark also established an Indian Museum in St. Louis in 1811, to teach people about Native Americans living in the West. The museum was located very close to where the Gateway Arch stands today. It also served as a place for meetings between Native Americans and representatives of the United States government.

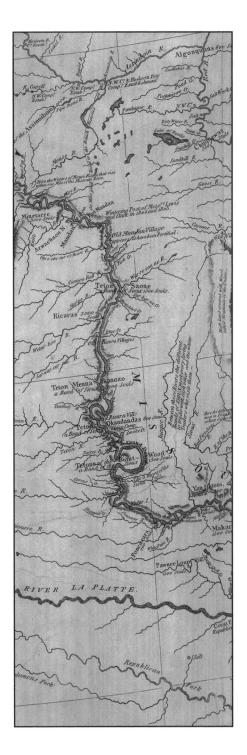

At right: part of a map made in 1814, based on William Clark's journal, showing the route of the Lewis and Clark expedition.

Chapter 3

Settlers Move West

Inspired by Lewis and Clark and other reports coming back from the West, many Americans headed west in the 19th century. Some of the first were fur trappers and traders looking to trade with the Native Americans for valuable furs. Used for fashionable clothing, the furs could be sold at high prices in the eastern United States and in Europe. The trappers and traders were soon followed by tens of thousands of settlers.

The Oregon Trail

Many Americans saw the "Oregon Country" in the Pacific Northwest as a good place to start new farms and settlements. The Oregon Country, partly explored by Lewis and Clark and claimed by the United States, was a large area including the present-day states of Oregon, Washington, and Idaho, as well as parts of Montana and Wyoming. Great Britain had also claimed this area, but an 1846 agreement gave it to the United States.

Beginning in the 1840s, tens of thousands of people packed up all of their belongings and headed west in wagon trains over the Oregon Trail.

Even before that, beginning in 1841 settlers began traveling to the Oregon Country over what became known as the Oregon Trail. This was a 2,000-mile (3,200-kilometer) wagon trail that stretched from Independence, Missouri, across the Great Plains and Rocky Mountains to Oregon. Part of the trail followed the route taken by Lewis and Clark.

Over the next 20 years more than 50,000 people used the trail to go west. Most of them traveled in wagon trains—it was safer for families to travel in a large group than alone. Each wagon train included a large number of covered wagons, and each covered wagon usually carried a family and all of its belongings.

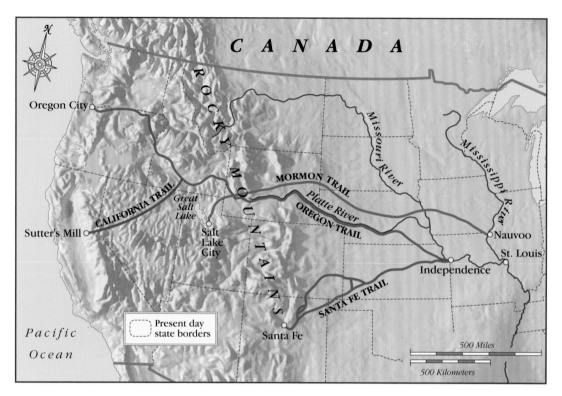

The Oregon Trail was just one of the routes settlers followed to reach different parts of the West in the 1800s.

The journey took about six months, so most wagon trains left at the beginning of spring, and the settlers hoped to arrive in Oregon before winter weather made it impossible to cross the Rockies. The journey was as hard as it was long. Travelers had to cross rough country and had to survive bad weather, lack of food and clean water, illnesses and injuries, and sometimes attacks by Native Americans. Some died, but most completed the journey successfully.

Other Trails West

The Santa Fe Trail was opened by trader William Becknell in 1821. It extended for about 800 miles (1,200 kilometers) between Missouri and the town of Santa Fe in New Mexico, which was then a part of Mexico. At first the trail was used mostly by traders. After the United States defeated Mexico in the Mexican-American War of 1846–1848, New Mexico became part of the United States. Beginning in the 1850s, many settlers also used the trail to move to the Southwest.

Over a period of about ten years starting in 1846, about 12,000 members of the Church of Jesus Christ of Latter-day Saints, called Mormons, journeyed from western Illinois to an area near the Great Salt Lake, in present-day Utah. The Mormons faced **persecution** in Illinois because of their religious beliefs. Following their leader, Brigham Young, they took a route now called the Mormon Trail to go west and establish a new society in the wilderness.

Gold Rush

The discovery of gold in northern California in 1848 created excitement all over the United States—and around the world. Once the news had spread, in 1849 tens of thousands of people hurried to California thinking they would quickly find gold and get rich. This event became known as the California Gold Rush. Many of the gold rushers, sometimes called "49ers,"

Abigail Scott Duniway (1834–1915)

Abigail Scott Duniway was one of the many Americans who migrated from the Midwest to Oregon on the Oregon Trail. Her family traveled from Illinois by covered wagon in 1852, when she was 17. The journey was so difficult that Duniway's mother and brother both died on the trip. Despite having little formal education, Duniway became a teacher and a writer of books about life in the West. In the late 19th century, she was a leader of the movement for equal rights for women, and her efforts helped women gain the right to vote in Oregon and other western states.

With all of their gear packed onto mules and in wagons, these 49ers in California head for what they hope will be a good spot to mine for gold—and strike it rich.

took ships to get to California. But as many as 40,000 traveled west in wagons. Most followed the Oregon Trail as far as Idaho. Then, they headed southwest on an overland route called the California Trail.

Most 49ers did not find gold or become rich, but many of them stayed in California anyway, becoming farmers and ranchers and establishing settlements. People continued to flock to California and other western states in search of gold and other valuable metals throughout the 1800s.

In Their Own Words

Laura Ingalls Wilder (1867–1957)

Laura Ingalls Wilder wrote popular children's books about what her childhood was like in the late 1800s. Her family often moved from place to place in a covered wagon. The places where they lived included Wisconsin, Iowa, Missouri, Kansas, and what is now Oklahoma. Wilder's books were about the value of hard work and keeping hope in hard times. They also described the misunderstandings that often occurred between white settlers and Native Americans. In this passage from her book *Little House on the Prairie*, Wilder describes the fear and curiosity she and her family felt for the Native Americans living around them in Indian Territory (in what is now Oklahoma):

> "Laura and [her sister] Mary ran to the window. They saw the Indian's straight back, riding away on a pony. He held a gun across his knees, its ends stuck out on either side of him…. 'Let Indians keep themselves to themselves,' said Ma, 'and we will do the same. I don't like Indians around underfoot.' Pa told her not to worry. 'That Indian was perfectly friendly,' he told her. 'And their camps down among the bluffs are peaceable enough. If we treat them well…we won't have any trouble.'"

Although Laura's father encouraged her mother not to fear the Native Americans living around them, such fears were very common. Many white settlers knew very little about Native Americans and had trouble understanding their different way of life.

This photo shows Laura Ingalls Wilder in 1884, when she was about seventeen years old.

A family on their Nebraska farm in the 1880s. Hundreds of thousands of Americans moved west in the second half of the 19th century to take advantage of the government's offer of free farmland.

The Homestead Act

Many other people traveled west after the U.S. Congress passed the Homestead Act in 1862. Under this law, the U.S. government gave any settler over 21 years of age 160 acres (65 hectares) of unsettled public land, as long as the settler lived on it and took care of it for at least five years. The idea of free land and a new life appealed to many workers who lived in large cities in the eastern United States and made little money. In the second half of the 19th century, at least 400,000 families moved west to live on and to farm land they got under the Homestead Act. Many of these families had a very hard time in their new lives. Some of the land was not very good for farming. Some of the settlers did not know a great deal about farming. And life in undeveloped areas was hard. But most people stayed in their new homes in the West and built a new life.

The Railroads

When Lewis and Clark began their expedition up the Missouri River, water travel was the best way to cover a long distance. That would change by the

Workers and others celebrated when the western and eastern sections of the first transcontinental railroad were joined together in 1869.

The Eads Bridge over the Mississippi, connecting St. Louis and Illinois, was one of the largest bridges that existed when it was completed in 1874.

Eads Bridge

The Eads Bridge in St. Louis was completed in 1874. It is named for the engineer who designed it, James Buchanan Eads. It was one of the first steel bridges to cross the Mississippi River, and it was also one of the largest bridges that existed at that time. Before it was built, ferries were used to cross the river between Illinois and St. Louis. Having the bridge meant that trains and wagons could cross the river much more safely and easily. The building of the bridge allowed St. Louis to continue to serve as a major gateway to the West.

mid-1800s with the expansion of the railroads. In the early 1800s railway lines were built to connect major eastern cities, such as New York and Boston. Plans to build railroads all the way to the Pacific Ocean were interrupted by the Civil War (1861–1865). By the end of the Civil War, railroads had reached Missouri and other parts of the Midwest.

The first "transcontinental" railroad, connecting the Midwest with California, was completed in 1869. Teams of railroad builders, one working west from Nebraska and one working east from California, met at the town of Promontory, Utah, on May 10, 1869. The tracks they had built were connected by a golden spike, and the first transcontinental railroad was ready to be used.

In the years that followed, other transcontinental railroad lines were built, and these railroads increased settlement of the American West. Not only could people travel more easily, but freight trains could carry manufactured goods from the East to the West and farm products in the other direction.

The Closing of the Frontier

Throughout its history, Americans thought of the United States as having a **frontier**—an imaginary dividing line between the settled eastern part of the country, in which most people lived, and a western area that was unsettled or being settled. Where the frontier was changed during the country's history, as the United States grew and more people moved west. When the U.S. government counted the number of Americans in the **census** of 1890, it found that nearly 63 million people lived in the United States. It also found that because so many **migrants** had moved to the western United States by that time, all parts of the country had been settled. The government announced that what had long been referred to as the frontier was closed—or no longer existed.

Designing and Building the Arch

D espite the important role St. Louis had played in westward expansion during the 1800s, by the 1930s parts of the city, including the riverfront area, were not prospering. The United States and the rest of the world were suffering through hard economic times in the 1930s (this period is known as the Great Depression). Many people had abandoned their homes and businesses near the St. Louis riverfront. Homeless people were living there.

The city's government and business leaders started looking for ways to improve the riverfront area. They began making plans to clear the area of its decaying buildings in order to build a monument there. A lawyer named Luther Ely Smith joined with Bernard Dickman, the mayor of St. Louis, to lead this effort. By 1935, Dickman and Smith joined with other St. Louis residents to form the Jefferson National Expansion Memorial Association (JNEMA). The association wanted

Chapter

4

A huge steel and concrete section is lifted to the top of the Arch during construction.

to establish a memorial park and monument to honor President Thomas Jefferson for his role in supporting westward expansion and for making the city of St. Louis so important in the development of the West.

Throughout the 1930s, Smith worked to raise money for the memorial. He even convinced the U.S. government and the city of St. Louis to pay for it. Still, his plans were delayed while the United States fought in World War II from 1941 to 1945.

Planning the Memorial

After World War II, JNEMA could again focus on planning its memorial to westward expansion. In 1947, leaders of the organization decided to hold

Announcing the Design Competition

Newspapers all over the United States printed articles about the design competition. In an article with the headline "Memorial to Hail Jefferson, West," the *New York Times* reported on March 30, 1947: "An architectural competition…to obtain a design for a $30,000,000 Federal memorial to Thomas Jefferson and the pioneers of the Western expansion of the United States was announced [in St. Louis] today." The article went on to report the prize money to be awarded, including $40,000 for the first place winner. The *Times* also described the memorial's purpose this way: "It is intended that the memorial area be developed as a place of resort, inspiration, relaxation, and instruction for visitors from all over the world."

Many people across the United States read announcements like this one. As news of the competition spread, more than 170 architects decided to enter.

a design competition, or contest, and to offer prize money to the **architect** who came up with the best design for the memorial.

JNEMA received 172 entries for its competition. The winner was an architect named Eero Saarinen. His design was a modern-looking arch to be made of stainless steel and concrete. He wanted the arch to take the shape of an inverted catenary curve—the same shape that a chain takes if it hangs down while held in the middle.

Saarinen's design came to be called the "Gateway Arch" because the shape appeared to represent a gateway to the West. The Gateway Arch would be a hollow stainless steel frame with an inside layer of concrete to support it.

Although it would be 630 feet (192 meters) tall—making it the tallest monument in the United States—it would be strong enough to withstand winds of up to 150 miles (240 kilometers) per hour. Because it would be hollow inside, something could be built to carry passengers to an **observatory** at the top.

Construction of the Arch was delayed again by the Korean War (1950–1953), as well as by the need to move a set of railroad tracks that ran along the riverfront. Finally, workers began digging the deep foundations for the Arch in 1961.

Building the Arch—A Dangerous Job

Building the Arch was a very dangerous job. Usually a **scaffold**—a platform that construction workers can stand on while they do much of their work—is used when a new building is being put up. But because of the Arch's unusual size and shape, using a normal scaffold was impossible. The workers who built the Arch often had to work high off the ground, sometimes in rain or high winds, without much to catch them if they fell. Fortunately, no workers were killed during the construction of the Arch.

This is one of the creeper derricks that ran on tracks up the sides of the Arch to lift heavy building materials.

Eero Saarinen (1910–1961)

Eero Saarinen was born in Finland on August 20, 1910. His family moved to the United States, to an area north of Detroit, Michigan, in 1922. Eero's father was a well-known architect named Eliel Saarinen. Eliel encouraged all of his children to draw, design, and create. Eero would later say that his parents had given him "above all, a love for work."

Eero studied sculpture in Paris and architecture at Yale University in New Haven, Connecticut. He became a partner at his father's design firm when he was 26. When they heard of the contest to design a St. Louis memorial honoring Thomas Jefferson, both Eliel and Eero sent in designs. Because the two Saarinens had the same last name, organizers of the competition mistakenly told Eliel that he had won. While the family was celebrating his win a few days later, a telegram arrived with an apology. It said that Eero had, in fact, been selected as the winner.

In addition to designing the Arch, Eero Saarinen designed very modern-looking buildings for large companies (including a famous group of buildings in Michigan for General Motors). He also designed buildings for colleges, as well as graceful airport terminal buildings that suggest flight.

Eero Saarinen died in 1961, in the same year that work finally began on the Arch. He never got to see his memorial to Jefferson once it had been completed.

Eero Saarinen is on the left in this photo, with a model of the Arch in front of him. The man on the right is another architect who worked with Saarinen.

Obstacles to Overcome

Both sides of the Arch were built at the same time, with the plan that they would eventually meet in the middle, at the very top. Even as construction began, though, architects and engineers were unsure of how they would be able to keep moving building materials further up the sides of the Arch. Most construction equipment could reach only so high, and it did not seem possible that large pieces of stainless steel could be raised several hundred feet up the sides of the Arch without some kind of new, special equipment.

This problem was solved after the development of devices called **creeper derricks**. Each of these large machines could move up one leg of the Arch on a track similar to a railroad track. In that way, they could carry the heavy building materials. Two creeper derricks were built, one to run on each leg of the Arch.

One Last Challenge

As work on the Arch neared completion, engineers found that they had one last challenge to face. They were worried that the two sides of the Arch might not fit together when the last piece was put in place at the top. Because the legs of the Arch were so heavy, they were starting to sag in toward the middle more than engineers had expected they would. To solve this problem, the engineers had workers run a long metal support between the two legs of the Arch. The support, called a **truss**, held the legs up so that they would be in the right position when the last piece was put in place.

The Arch was finally completed on October 28, 1965. Many residents of St. Louis watched the event live on television, and many more people around the country watched pictures of it on the evening news. Hundreds of people also gathered on the riverfront next to the Arch to witness the historic moment.

Eyes of the Nation on St. Louis

Because it had taken so many years to plan, raise funds for, design, and finally start construction of the Gateway Arch, Americans watched closely as it was built in the 1960s. Just a few days before the last piece of the Arch was put in place, the *New York Times* published an article on October 24, 1965, about how much hard work the project had taken. It jokingly compared the hardships faced by the Arch organizers with those that pioneers had faced in the 19th century:

> "St. Louis's soaring Gateway Arch, a 630-foot stainless steel memorial to the pioneers who moved West across the Mississippi River here, comes to what construction men call the 'topping out' stage next week....
>
> "The 'topping out' will mark a triumph over problems of design, engineering, and construction and also over financial and organizational perils that rivaled the hazards of the pioneers whose hardihood the arch honors."

The *New York Times* was not the only newspaper (or magazine) to point out how long it was taking to build the Arch. Still, architects and engineers remained confident that people would be impressed with the Arch when it was completed.

The last piece of the Arch is put in place on October 28, 1965.

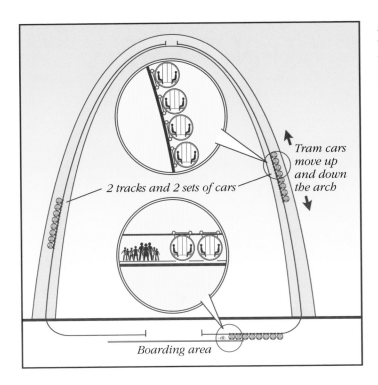

2 tracks and 2 sets of cars

Tram cars
move up
and down
the arch

Boarding area

A special tram system
was created to get
visitors to the top of
the Arch.

Tram Cars to the Top

Although the outside of the Arch was completed in 1965, it would take two
more years to build a system to take visitors to the top of the monument.
For years engineers had been unsure of how to do this. It would be too difficult for many visitors to climb stairs all the way to the top. But because
the Arch was curved, a normal elevator—meaning one that moved straight
up and down—could not be used.

It was Richard Bowser, an inventor and designer of elevator systems,
who had the idea of using a tram system, which would combine aspects of
a train and an elevator. Two trams were constructed inside of the Arch—one
in each leg. Each tram was made up of 8 cars linked together—much like
the cars on a train. Each was powered by an elevator engine. The trams
were completed in 1967, finally allowing visitors the chance to reach the top
of the Arch.

Visiting the Arch Today

The Gateway Arch is just one part of the Jefferson National Expansion Memorial. This memorial is run by the U.S. National Park Service. It covers 91 acres (37 hectares) of land on the Mississippi riverfront. Most of the memorial is made up of a park. Visitors walking through the park can look at the Arch from several different angles. The park also provides stunning views of the Mississippi River and of downtown St. Louis. Other parts of the memorial are the Museum of Westward Expansion and St. Louis's historic Old Courthouse.

The Old Courthouse

The Old Courthouse, just across the street from the Gateway Arch, was completed in 1828. It was expanded in 1839. The building played an important role in the national debate about African-American slavery in the United States before the Civil War. Until

St. Louis's historic Old Courthouse (the white building in the center of the photo) as seen from the top of the Gateway Arch. The Arch's shadow on the ground can also be seen in the photo.

The Dred Scott Decision

Dred Scott was a slave owned by a U.S. Army surgeon. He first sued for his freedom in St. Louis's Old Courthouse in 1847. For a time his master had taken him to Illinois and Wisconsin, where slavery was illegal, and Scott argued that he had become free while outside Missouri. Scott lost the first trial, but he sued again in 1850 and won. His owner appealed the decision to higher courts, and in 1857 the case reached the U.S. Supreme Court. In a decision that upset people who opposed slavery in the United States, the Supreme Court ruled that Scott could not sue for his freedom because a slave could not be a U.S. citizen. It also ruled that slaves were property owned by their masters, so Scott could not have been freed by being taken out of Missouri. The decision disappointed people who hoped that slavery in the United States could be ended peacefully. In the 1860s, slavery was ended by the Civil War.

the Civil War, slavery was legal in Missouri, and at times slaves were sold on the steps of the courthouse. In 1847 and again in 1850 the courthouse was the scene of trials in the historic case of Dred Scott, a slave whose attempt to sue for his freedom reached the U.S. Supreme Court.

The Museum of Westward Expansion

The Museum of Westward Expansion first opened in 1976—11 years after the completion of the outside of the Arch. The museum is located underneath the Arch. Visitors walk down several steps to get to it. The museum is in the shape of a semi-circle, and visitors are able to walk past displays about U.S. history and everyday life in the years between 1800 and 1900. Events that happened during these years are illustrated with photographs and paintings. The museum also has an exhibit dedicated to the Lewis and Clark expedition. At the center of the museum are items such as beads, clothing, tobacco, tipis, and covered wagons. These things belonged to

At the Museum of Westward Expansion, visitors can see displays about life in the West in the 1800s.

In Their Own Words

Susan Saarinen on the Gateway Arch

Eero Saarinen's daughter Susan grew up watching her father work on the Gateway Arch. Years after her father's death and the completion of the Arch, she explained how she finally learned to appreciate its importance:

> "My father won the Jefferson National Expansion Memorial Competition in 1948. I was three years old. I grew up with chains hanging in the basement, complex mechanical drawings on the drafting board, and a model of the tram car to climb in and out of. It didn't occur to me at the time that the Arch was special. It was simply my father's job.... Today I have completely different feelings. My brother and I...can step back and look at the Arch; at all it means and what it took to put it there and really appreciate it. We can look up and say 'WOW!'"

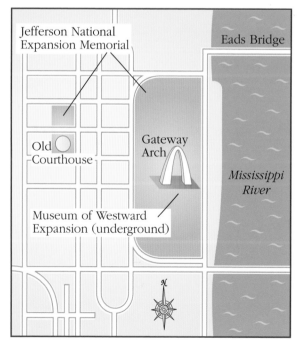

Native Americans and to pioneers who traveled West—and they help visitors understand what life was like for these people.

Going to the Top

Almost a million people a year ride the trams to the top of the Arch. Each of the two trams has eight cars for riders, and there are five

The Jefferson National Expansion Memorial includes the Gateway Arch, the Museum of Westward Expansion, the Old Courthouse, and a beautiful park on the Mississippi River.

At the top of the Arch, visitors lean forward to enjoy the best views out the windows.

seats in each car. It takes about 4 minutes for a tram to travel to the top of the Arch and 3 minutes for it to travel back down again.

Some visitors who are afraid of heights decide not to go to the top of the Arch. Those who do make the 4-minute trip up to the observatory can look through the windows at the top and get a great view of downtown St. Louis on one side and of the Mississippi River and the state of Illinois on the other side.

The Gateway Arch today remains a graceful and elegant reminder of the American push for westward expansion. The Arch and the larger Jefferson National Expansion Memorial have improved the riverfront area and become one of the most popular tourist attractions in St. Louis. The Arch and the memorial remind visitors of the growth and expansion of the United States in the 1800s, starting with Thomas Jefferson's bold decision to make the Louisiana Purchase. They also serve as a reminder of the importance of the city of St. Louis as a gateway to the American West.

Timeline ★ ★ ★ ★ ★ ★ ★ ★ ★

★ **1803**   Under President Thomas Jefferson, the United States makes the Louisiana Purchase from France.

★ **1804–1806** The Lewis and Clark Expedition explores part of the Louisiana Purchase and goes beyond to the Pacific Ocean.

★ **1807**   Fur traders and other explorers begin to head west in growing numbers.

★ **1841**   Settlers begin traveling to the Pacific Northwest over the Oregon Trail.

★ **1846**   Mormons begin migrating to Utah over the Mormon Trail.

★ **1848**   In the treaty ending the Mexican-American War, Mexico turns over to the United States a large amount of land in the Southwest.

★ **1849**   The Gold Rush draws tens of thousands of people to northern California.

★ **1862**   Congress passes the Homestead Act, giving free land in the West to new settlers.

★ **1869**   The first transcontinental railroad is completed

★ **1890**   The U.S. government announces that the country has become completely settled and the frontier is closed.

★ **1935**   Leaders in St. Louis decide to build a memorial to honor Thomas Jefferson and westward expansion.

★ **1947**   A design competition for the memorial is announced.

★ **1948**   Architect Eero Saarinen's arch design wins the memorial design competition.

★ **1961**   Construction of the Gateway Arch begins.

★ **1965**   The outside of the Gateway Arch is completed.

★ **1967**   The tram system inside the Gateway Arch is completed, and visitors can travel to the top for the first time.

★ **1976**   The Museum of Westward Expansions, located underneath the Arch, opens.

agent: Someone who handles matters for another person.

arch: A curved structure with two legs.

architect: A person who designs buildings and other structures and who understands how they are built.

census: An official count of the number of people living in an area.

continental United States: The part of the United States that is on the continent of North America (all U.S. states except Hawaii).

creeper derricks: Large machines that carried building materials to the top of the Arch by running on tracks up the sides.

crest: The top of something, such as a mountain or mountain range.

expedition: A journey for a specific purpose.

frontier: An undeveloped area of land on the edge of a settled area.

gateway: An entrance.

inverted catenary curve: The shape that a chain takes when it is held in the center and the two sides hang down.

migrants: People who move from one place to another.

monument: A structure put up to remember a special person or event.

national memorial: A landmark or other place set aside by the U.S. government because of its historic importance.

observatory: A place to observe, or see, something.

persecution: Treating people badly or harming them, often because of their race or religion.

pioneers: The first people to settle a new land or territory.

prairie: A large area of land with tall grasses and few trees.

reservation: An area of land set aside for Native Americans to live on.

scaffold: A platform that supports construction workers.

truss: A metal beam placed between the legs of the Arch to keep them from sagging inward during construction.

wilderness: An area that has not been widely settled or developed by human beings.

To Learn More ★ ★ ★ ★ ★ ★ ★

Read these books

Josephson, Judith Pinkerton. *Growing Up in Pioneer America, 1800 to 1890*. Minneapolis: Lerner Publications, 2003.

Kukla, Amy, and Jon Kukla. *Thomas Jefferson: Life, Liberty, and the Pursuit of Happiness*. New York: PowerPlus Books, 2005.

Orr, Tamra. *The Lewis and Clark Expedition: A Primary Source History of the Journey of the Corps of Discovery*. New York: Rosen Publishing, 2004.

Sonneborn, Liz. *The Shoshones*. Minneapolis: Lerner Publications, 2007.

Steele, Christy, and Ann Hodgson, eds. *A Covered Wagon Girl: The Diary of Sally Hester, 1849–1850*. Mankato, Minn.: Blue Earth Books, 2000.

Steele, Christy. *The Louisiana Purchase*. Milwaukee: World Almanac Library, 2005.

Look up these Web sites

Gateway Arch Riverfront
http://www.gatewayarch.com/Arch

Jefferson National Expansion Memorial
http://www.nps.gov/jeff

Lewis and Clark Journey of Discovery
http://www.nps.gov/archive/jeff/LewisClark2/HomePage/HomePage.htm

Museum of Westward Expansion
http://www.nps.gov/jeff/planyourvisit/museum-of-westward-expansion.htm

The Old Courthouse
http://www.nps.gov/archive/jeff/courthouse.html

Key Internet search terms

Gateway Arch, Lewis and Clark, Louisiana Purchase, Oregon Trail, St. Louis

The abbreviation *ill.* stands for illustration, and *ills.* stands for illustrations. Page references to illustrations and maps are in *italic* type.

Index ★ ★ ★ ★ ★ ★ ★ ★ ★ ★

★ ★

About the Author

Chelsey Hankins grew up in central Illinois and used to visit the Gateway
Arch almost every summer with her family. She holds a B.A. from the
University of Illinois, Urbana-Champaign and an M.A. from The Ohio State
University, both in American history. She lives in Chicago, where she works
as a research editor and a freelance writer and fact-checker.

1